Special Thank You To:

Alyssa Ashley for your AMAZING artwork!

Preparation is EVERYTHING!

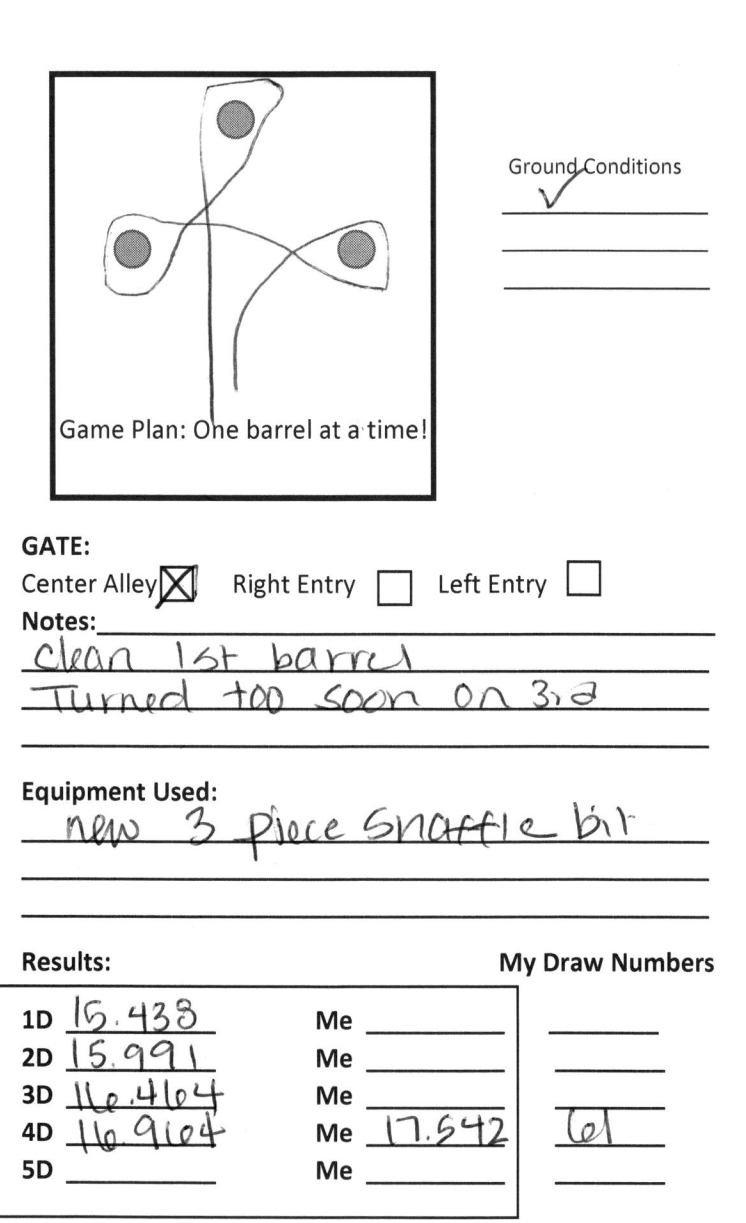

Game Plan: One barrel at a time!

Ground Conditions
✓
_____
_____
_____

GATE:
Center Alley ☒   Right Entry ☐   Left Entry ☐

Notes:
Clean 1st barrel
Turned too soon on 3rd
_____

Equipment Used:
new 3 piece snaffle bit
_____
_____

Results: **My Draw Numbers**

1D 15.438	Me _____	_____
2D 15.991	Me _____	_____
3D 16.464	Me _____	_____
4D 16.904	Me 17.542	61
5D _____	Me _____	_____

TEAM YEAGER
www.AprilYeager.org

Entry Log

When people ask "what do you do", your answer should be "Whatever it takes".

Rodeo ☐   Jackpot ☒

Location - **Kukas**

Date & Time **10/24 7pm**

Association _____ Added Money _____ Entry Fee **$30 + $5 fee**

How Many Entries **1**

Balance Sheet:

Horse	Money Won	Entry Fee Per
Earl		$40

Miles to Arena _____ Multiply by 2 _____
Vehicle Average MPG _____
Fuel Price Per Gallon _____
Hauling Partner(s) _____

Travel Cost to Show:

Enter miles to arena times 2. Divide MPG into mileage. Multiply outcome by the price per gallon. If you have hauling partners divide by that number. If you want cost per horse you can divide by the number of horses in the trailer.

$ _____   **Profit/Loss $ _____**

Stalls _____
Lodging _____
Other _____

Thankful, grateful, blessed! Doing what I love and loving what I do!!

TEAM YEAGER
www.AprilYeager.org

Preparation is EVERYTHING!

only →

Game Plan: One barrel at a time!

Ground Conditions
_____
_____
_____

GATE:
Center Alley ☐   Right Entry ☐   Left Entry ☒

Notes: _Tiny pattern, tough approach to first_

Equipment Used: _Snaffle_

Results: **My Draw Numbers**

1D _13.499_   Me _____
2D _14.023_   Me _14.431_   _20_
3D _14.57_   Me _____
4D _15.039_   Me _____
5D _____   Me _____

TEAM YEAGER
www.AprilYeager.org

Entry Log

When people ask "what do you do", your answer should be "Whatever it takes".

Rodeo ☐   Jackpot ☒

Location - _Devoted K_

Date & Time _2/16 1pm_

Association _____ Added Money _____ Entry Fee _____
How Many Entries _1_

Balance Sheet:

Horse	Money Won	Entry Fee Per
Earl		$45

Miles to Arena _____   Multiply by 2 _____
Vehicle Average MPG _____
Fuel Price Per Gallon _____
Hauling Partner(s) _____

Travel Cost to Show:

Enter miles to arena times 2. Divide MPG into mileage. Multiply outcome by the price per gallon. If you have hauling partners divide by that number. If you want cost per horse you can divide by the number of horses in the trailer.

$_____   **Profit/Loss $_____**

Stalls _____
Lodging _____
Other _____

Thankful, grateful, blessed! Doing what I love and loving what I do!!

TEAM YEAGER
www.AprilYeager.org

Preparation is EVERYTHING!

Game Plan: One barrel at a time!

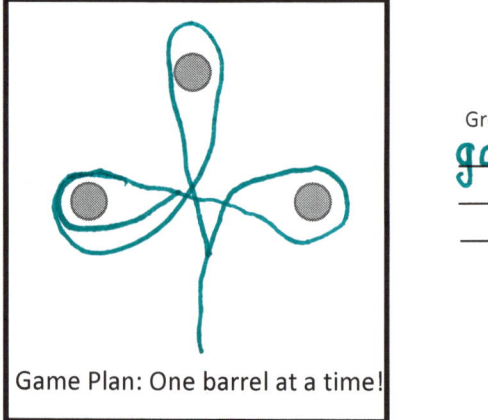

Ground Conditions
good

GATE:
Center Alley [X]   Right Entry [ ]   Left Entry [ ]

Notes: velvet

Equipment Used:

Results: **My Draw Numbers**

1D _____	Me 22.300
2D _____	Me _____
3D _____	Me _____
4D _____	Me _____
5D _____	Me _____

TEAM YEAGER
www.AprilYeager.org

Entry Log

When people ask "what do you do", your answer should be "Whatever it takes".

Rodeo ☒ Jackpot ☐

Location - **Granite falls**

Date & Time
_____

Association _____ Added Money _____ Entry Fee _____
How Many Entries _____

Balance Sheet:

Horse	Money Won	Entry Fee Per
velvet	48$	310$

Miles to Arena _____ Multiply by 2 _____
Vehicle Average MPG _____
Fuel Price Per Gallon _____
Hauling Partner(s) _____
Travel Cost to Show:
Enter miles to arena times 2. Divide MPG into mileage. Multiply outcome by the price per gallon. If you have hauling partners divide by that number. If you want cost per horse you can divide by the number of horses in the trailer.

$ _____ **Profit/Loss** $ _____
Stalls _____
Lodging _____
Other _____

Thankful, grateful, blessed! Doing what I love and loving what I do!!

TEAM YEAGER
www.AprilYeager.org

Preparation is EVERYTHING!

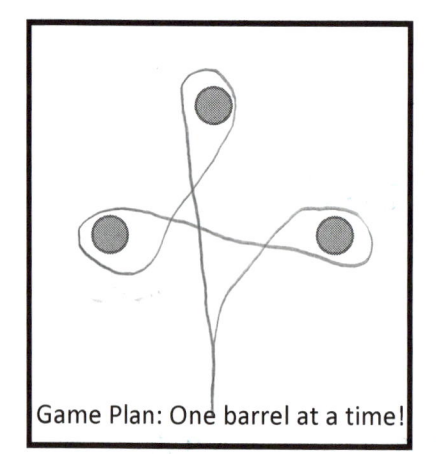

Game Plan: One barrel at a time!

Ground Conditions: Perfect

GATE:
Center Alley [X]   Right Entry [ ]   Left Entry [ ]

Notes: I ran to wide around my 1rst and second barrel

Equipment Used:

Results: **My Draw Numbers**

1D	_____	Me	19.9
2D	_____	Me	_____
3D	_____	Me	19.9
4D	_____	Me	_____
5D	_____	Me	_____

TEAM YEAGER
www.AprilYeager.org

Entry Log

When people ask "what do you do", your answer should be "Whatever it takes".

Rodeo ☒   Jackpot ☐

Location - Prinston

Date & Time _____

Association Lit(brit) Added Money none Entry Fee $300

How Many Entries odels

Balance Sheet:

Horse	Money Won	Entry Fee Per
Hank	$20	

Miles to Arena _____   Multiply by 2 _____
Vehicle Average MPG _____
Fuel Price Per Gallon _____
Hauling Partner(s) _____
Travel Cost to Show:
Enter miles to arena times 2. Divide MPG into mileage. Multiply outcome by the price per gallon. If you have hauling partners divide by that number. If you want cost per horse you can divide by the number of horses in the trailer.

$ _____   **Profit/Loss** $ _____
Stalls _____
Lodging _____
Other _____

Thankful, grateful, blessed! Doing what I love and loving what I do!!

TEAM YEAGER
www.AprilYeager.org

Preparation is EVERYTHING!

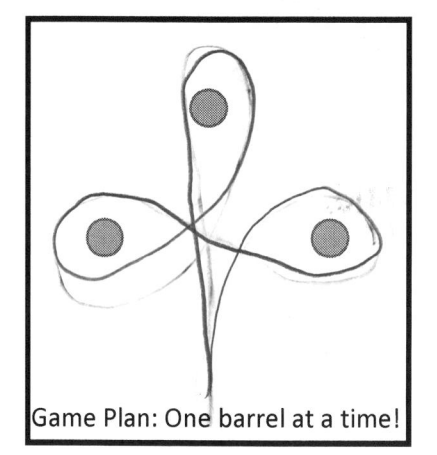

Game Plan: One barrel at a time!

Ground Conditions
_____
_____
_____

GATE:
Center Alley ☐   Right Entry ☐   Left Entry ☐
Notes: _kick hole way, do not pull back until past timer line_
_____
_____

Equipment Used:
_____
_____
_____

Results: **My Draw Numbers**

1D _____   Me _____   _____
2D _____   Me _____   _____
3D _____   Me _____   _____
4D _____   Me _____   _____
5D _____   Me _20 & 5_   _____

TEAM YEAGER
www.AprilYeager.org

Entry Log

When people ask "what do you do", your answer should be "Whatever it takes".

Rodeo ☐   Jackpot ☒

Location - ___J and S arena___

Date & Time
_____

Association _____ Added Money _____ Entry Fee _____
How Many Entries _____

Balance Sheet:

Horse	Money Won	Entry Fee Per
Dixie		

Miles to Arena _____ Multiply by 2 _____
Vehicle Average MPG _____
Fuel Price Per Gallon _____
Hauling Partner(s) _____

Travel Cost to Show:

Enter miles to arena times 2. Divide MPG into mileage. Multiply outcome by the price per gallon. If you have hauling partners divide by that number. If you want cost per horse you can divide by the number of horses in the trailer.

$ _____   **Profit/Loss $ _____**

Stalls _____
Lodging _____
Other _____

Thankful, grateful, blessed! Doing what I love and loving what I do!!

TEAM YEAGER
www.AprilYeager.org

Preparation is EVERYTHING!

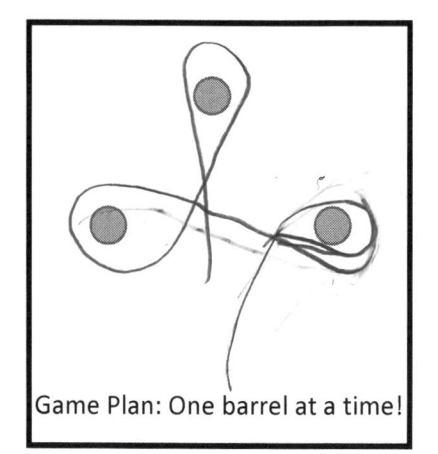

Game Plan: One barrel at a time!

Ground Conditions
_____
_____
_____

GATE:
Center Alley ☐   Right Entry ☐   Left Entry ☐
Notes: _reach down and turn_
_on first barrel_____
_____
_____

Equipment Used:
_____
_____
_____

Results: **My Draw Numbers**

1D _____	Me _____ (no time)	_____
2D _____	Me _____	_____
3D _____	Me _____	_____
4D _____	Me _____	_____
5D _____	Me _____	_____

TEAM YEAGER
www.AprilYeager.org

Entry Log

When people ask "what do you do", your answer should be "Whatever it takes".

Rodeo ☐   Jackpot ☐

Location -
_____
Date & Time
_____
Association _____ Added Money _____ Entry Fee _____
How Many Entries _____

Balance Sheet:

Horse	Money Won	Entry Fee Per
Mojo		

Miles to Arena_____ Multiply by 2_____
Vehicle Average MPG_____
Fuel Price Per Gallon_____
Hauling Partner(s)_____

Travel Cost to Show:

Enter miles to arena times 2. Divide MPG into mileage. Multiply outcome by the price per gallon. If you have hauling partners divide by that number. If you want cost per horse you can divide by the number of horses in the trailer.

$_____   **Profit/Loss $_____**

Stalls _____
Lodging _____
Other _____

Thankful, grateful, blessed! Doing what I love and loving what I do!!

TEAM YEAGER
www.AprilYeager.org

Preparation is EVERYTHING!

Game Plan: One barrel at a time!

Ground Conditions
_____
_____
_____

GATE:
Center Alley ☐   Right Entry ☐   Left Entry ☐

Notes: _____
_____
_____
_____

Equipment Used:
_____
_____
_____

Results: **My Draw Numbers**

1D _____	Me _____	_____
2D _____	Me _____	_____
3D _____	Me _____	_____
4D _____	Me _____	_____
5D _____	Me _____	_____

TEAM YEAGER
www.AprilYeager.org

Entry Log

When people ask "what do you do", your answer should be "Whatever it takes".

Rodeo ☐   Jackpot ☐

Location -
_____

Date & Time
_____

Association _____ Added Money _____ Entry Fee _____
How Many Entries _____

Balance Sheet:

Horse	Money Won	Entry Fee Per

Miles to Arena _____ Multiply by 2 _____
Vehicle Average MPG _____
Fuel Price Per Gallon _____
Hauling Partner(s) _____
Travel Cost to Show:

Enter miles to arena times 2. Divide MPG into mileage. Multiply outcome by the price per gallon. If you have hauling partners divide by that number. If you want cost per horse you can divide by the number of horses in the trailer.

$ _____   **Profit/Loss $ _____**

Stalls _____
Lodging _____
Other _____

Thankful, grateful, blessed! Doing what I love and loving what I do!!

TEAM YEAGER
www.AprilYeager.org

Preparation is EVERYTHING!

Game Plan: One barrel at a time!

Ground Conditions
_____
_____
_____

GATE:
Center Alley ☐   Right Entry ☐   Left Entry ☐

Notes: _____
_____
_____
_____

Equipment Used:
_____
_____
_____

Results: **My Draw Numbers**

1D _____   Me _____   _____
2D _____   Me _____   _____
3D _____   Me _____   _____
4D _____   Me _____   _____
5D _____   Me _____   _____

TEAM YEAGER
www.AprilYeager.org

Entry Log

When people ask "what do you do", your answer should be "Whatever it takes".

Rodeo ☐   Jackpot ☐

Location -

_____

Date & Time

_____

Association _____ Added Money _____ Entry Fee _____

How Many Entries _____

Balance Sheet:

Horse	Money Won	Entry Fee Per

Miles to Arena _____   Multiply by 2 _____

Vehicle Average MPG _____

Fuel Price Per Gallon _____

Hauling Partner(s) _____

Travel Cost to Show:

Enter miles to arena times 2. Divide MPG into mileage. Multiply outcome by the price per gallon. If you have hauling partners divide by that number. If you want cost per horse you can divide by the number of horses in the trailer.

$_____   **Profit/Loss $_____**

Stalls _____

Lodging _____

Other _____

Thankful, grateful, blessed! Doing what I love and loving what I do!!

TEAM YEAGER

www.AprilYeager.org

Preparation is EVERYTHING!

Game Plan: One barrel at a time!

Ground Conditions
_____
_____
_____

GATE:
Center Alley ☐   Right Entry ☐   Left Entry ☐

Notes: _____
_____
_____
_____

Equipment Used:
_____
_____
_____

Results: **My Draw Numbers**

1D _____	Me _____	_____
2D _____	Me _____	_____
3D _____	Me _____	_____
4D _____	Me _____	_____
5D _____	Me _____	_____

TEAM YEAGER
www.AprilYeager.org

Entry Log

When people ask "what do you do", your answer should be "Whatever it takes".

Rodeo ☐   Jackpot ☐

Location -

_____
Date & Time

_____
Association _____ Added Money_____ Entry Fee_____
How Many Entries _____

Balance Sheet:

Horse	Money Won	Entry Fee Per

Miles to Arena_____   Multiply by 2_____
Vehicle Average MPG_____
Fuel Price Per Gallon_____
Hauling Partner(s)_____
Travel Cost to Show:

Enter miles to arena times 2. Divide MPG into mileage. Multiply outcome by the price per gallon. If you have hauling partners divide by that number. If you want cost per horse you can divide by the number of horses in the trailer.

$_____   **Profit/Loss $_____**

Stalls _____
Lodging_____
Other_____

Thankful, grateful, blessed! Doing what I love and loving what I do!!

TEAM YEAGER
www.AprilYeager.org

Preparation is EVERYTHING!

Ground Conditions
_____
_____
_____

Game Plan: One barrel at a time!

GATE:
Center Alley ☐   Right Entry ☐   Left Entry ☐

Notes: _____
_____
_____
_____

Equipment Used:
_____
_____
_____

Results: **My Draw Numbers**

1D _____	Me _____	_____
2D _____	Me _____	_____
3D _____	Me _____	_____
4D _____	Me _____	_____
5D _____	Me _____	_____

TEAM YEAGER
www.AprilYeager.org

Entry Log

When people ask "what do you do", your answer should be "Whatever it takes".

Rodeo ☐   Jackpot ☐

Location -
_____

Date & Time
_____

Association _____ Added Money _____ Entry Fee _____

How Many Entries _____

Balance Sheet:

Horse	Money Won	Entry Fee Per

Miles to Arena _____ Multiply by 2 _____

Vehicle Average MPG _____

Fuel Price Per Gallon _____

Hauling Partner(s) _____

Travel Cost to Show:

Enter miles to arena times 2. Divide MPG into mileage. Multiply outcome by the price per gallon. If you have hauling partners divide by that number. If you want cost per horse you can divide by the number of horses in the trailer.

$ _____   **Profit/Loss $** _____

Stalls _____

Lodging _____

Other _____

Thankful, grateful, blessed! Doing what I love and loving what I do!!

TEAM YEAGER
www.AprilYeager.org

Preparation is EVERYTHING!

Game Plan: One barrel at a time!

Ground Conditions
_____
_____
_____

GATE:
Center Alley ☐   Right Entry ☐   Left Entry ☐

Notes: _____
_____
_____
_____

Equipment Used:
_____
_____
_____

Results: **My Draw Numbers**

1D _____	Me _____	_____
2D _____	Me _____	_____
3D _____	Me _____	_____
4D _____	Me _____	_____
5D _____	Me _____	_____

TEAM YEAGER
www.AprilYeager.org

Entry Log

When people ask "what do you do", your answer should be "Whatever it takes".

Rodeo ☐   Jackpot ☐

Location -
_____
Date & Time
_____
Association _____ Added Money _____ Entry Fee _____
How Many Entries _____

Balance Sheet:

Horse	Money Won	Entry Fee Per

Miles to Arena _____ Multiply by 2 _____
Vehicle Average MPG _____
Fuel Price Per Gallon _____
Hauling Partner(s) _____
Travel Cost to Show:

Enter miles to arena times 2. Divide MPG into mileage. Multiply outcome by the price per gallon. If you have hauling partners divide by that number. If you want cost per horse you can divide by the number of horses in the trailer.

$ _____   **Profit/Loss $ _____**

Stalls _____
Lodging _____
Other _____

Thankful, grateful, blessed! Doing what I love and loving what I do!!

TEAM YEAGER
www.AprilYeager.org

Preparation is EVERYTHING!

Game Plan: One barrel at a time!

Ground Conditions
_____
_____
_____

GATE:
Center Alley ☐   Right Entry ☐   Left Entry ☐

Notes: _____
_____
_____
_____

Equipment Used:
_____
_____
_____

Results: **My Draw Numbers**

1D _____	Me _____	_____
2D _____	Me _____	_____
3D _____	Me _____	_____
4D _____	Me _____	_____
5D _____	Me _____	

TEAM YEAGER
www.AprilYeager.org

Entry Log

When people ask "what do you do", your answer should be "Whatever it takes".

Rodeo ☐   Jackpot ☐

Location -
_____

Date & Time
_____

Association _____ Added Money _____ Entry Fee _____
How Many Entries _____

Balance Sheet:

Horse	Money Won	Entry Fee Per

Miles to Arena _____ Multiply by 2 _____
Vehicle Average MPG _____
Fuel Price Per Gallon _____
Hauling Partner(s) _____
Travel Cost to Show:

Enter miles to arena times 2. Divide MPG into mileage. Multiply outcome by the price per gallon. If you have hauling partners divide by that number. If you want cost per horse you can divide by the number of horses in the trailer.

$_____   **Profit/Loss $_____**

Stalls _____
Lodging _____
Other _____

Thankful, grateful, blessed! Doing what I love and loving what I do!!

TEAM YEAGER
www.AprilYeager.org

Preparation is EVERYTHING!

Game Plan: One barrel at a time!

Ground Conditions
_____
_____
_____

GATE:
Center Alley ☐   Right Entry ☐   Left Entry ☐

Notes: _____
_____
_____
_____

Equipment Used:
_____
_____
_____

Results:　　　　　　　　　　　　　　**My Draw Numbers**

1D _____	Me _____	_____
2D _____	Me _____	_____
3D _____	Me _____	_____
4D _____	Me _____	_____
5D _____	Me _____	

TEAM YEAGER
www.AprilYeager.org

Entry Log

When people ask "what do you do", your answer should be "Whatever it takes".

Rodeo ☐   Jackpot ☐

Location -
_____
Date & Time
_____
Association _____ Added Money _____ Entry Fee _____
How Many Entries _____

Balance Sheet:

Horse	Money Won	Entry Fee Per

Miles to Arena _____   Multiply by 2 _____
Vehicle Average MPG _____
Fuel Price Per Gallon _____
Hauling Partner(s) _____

Travel Cost to Show:

Enter miles to arena times 2. Divide MPG into mileage. Multiply outcome by the price per gallon. If you have hauling partners divide by that number. If you want cost per horse you can divide by the number of horses in the trailer.

$_____   **Profit/Loss $_____**

Stalls _____
Lodging _____
Other _____

Thankful, grateful, blessed! Doing what I love and loving what I do!!

TEAM YEAGER
www.AprilYeager.org

Preparation is EVERYTHING!

Game Plan: One barrel at a time!

Ground Conditions
_____
_____
_____

GATE:
Center Alley ☐   Right Entry ☐   Left Entry ☐

Notes: _____
_____
_____
_____

Equipment Used:
_____
_____
_____

Results: **My Draw Numbers**

1D _____	Me _____	_____
2D _____	Me _____	_____
3D _____	Me _____	_____
4D _____	Me _____	_____
5D _____	Me _____	_____

TEAM YEAGER
www.AprilYeager.org

Entry Log

When people ask "what do you do", your answer should be "Whatever it takes".

Rodeo ☐   Jackpot ☐

Location -
_____
Date & Time
_____
Association _____ Added Money _____ Entry Fee _____
How Many Entries _____

Balance Sheet:

Horse	Money Won	Entry Fee Per

Miles to Arena _____   Multiply by 2 _____
Vehicle Average MPG _____
Fuel Price Per Gallon _____
Hauling Partner(s) _____

Travel Cost to Show:

Enter miles to arena times 2. Divide MPG into mileage. Multiply outcome by the price per gallon. If you have hauling partners divide by that number. If you want cost per horse you can divide by the number of horses in the trailer.

$_____   **Profit/Loss $_____**

Stalls _____
Lodging _____
Other _____

Thankful, grateful, blessed! Doing what I love and loving what I do!!

TEAM YEAGER
www.AprilYeager.org

Preparation is EVERYTHING!

Game Plan: One barrel at a time!

Ground Conditions
_____
_____
_____

GATE:
Center Alley ☐   Right Entry ☐   Left Entry ☐

Notes: _____
_____
_____
_____

Equipment Used:
_____
_____
_____

Results: **My Draw Numbers**

1D _____	Me _____	_____
2D _____	Me _____	_____
3D _____	Me _____	_____
4D _____	Me _____	_____
5D _____	Me _____	_____

TEAM YEAGER
www.AprilYeager.org

Entry Log

When people ask "what do you do", your answer should be "Whatever it takes".

Rodeo ☐ Jackpot ☐

Location -
_____

Date & Time
_____

Association _____ Added Money _____ Entry Fee _____
How Many Entries _____

Balance Sheet:

Horse	Money Won	Entry Fee Per

Miles to Arena _____ Multiply by 2 _____
Vehicle Average MPG _____
Fuel Price Per Gallon _____
Hauling Partner(s) _____

Travel Cost to Show:

Enter miles to arena times 2. Divide MPG into mileage. Multiply outcome by the price per gallon. If you have hauling partners divide by that number. If you want cost per horse you can divide by the number of horses in the trailer.

$ _____   **Profit/Loss** $ _____
Stalls _____
Lodging _____
Other _____

Thankful, grateful, blessed! Doing what I love and loving what I do!!

TEAM YEAGER
www.AprilYeager.org

Preparation is EVERYTHING!

Ground Conditions
_____
_____
_____

Game Plan: One barrel at a time

GATE:
Center Alley ☐   Right Entry ☐   Left Entry ☐

Notes: _____
_____
_____
_____

Equipment Used:
_____
_____
_____

Results: **My Draw Numbers**

1D _____	Me _____	_____
2D _____	Me _____	_____
3D _____	Me _____	_____
4D _____	Me _____	_____
5D _____	Me _____	_____

TEAM YEAGER
www.AprilYeager.org

Entry Log

When people ask "what do you do", your answer should be "Whatever it takes".

Rodeo ☐ Jackpot ☐

Location -
_____

Date & Time
_____

Association _____ Added Money _____ Entry Fee _____
How Many Entries _____

Balance Sheet:

Horse	Money Won	Entry Fee Per

Miles to Arena _____ Multiply by 2 _____
Vehicle Average MPG _____
Fuel Price Per Gallon _____
Hauling Partner(s) _____
Travel Cost to Show:

Enter miles to arena times 2. Divide MPG into mileage. Multiply outcome by the price per gallon. If you have hauling partners divide by that number. If you want cost per horse you can divide by the number of horses in the trailer.

$ _____   **Profit/Loss $ _____**

Stalls _____
Lodging _____
Other _____

Thankful, grateful, blessed! Doing what I love and loving what I do!!

TEAM YEAGER
www.AprilYeager.org

Preparation is EVERYTHING!

Game Plan: One barrel at a time!

Ground Conditions
_____
_____
_____

GATE:
Center Alley ☐   Right Entry ☐   Left Entry ☐

Notes: _____
_____
_____
_____

Equipment Used:
_____
_____
_____

Results: **My Draw Numbers**

1D _____	Me _____	_____
2D _____	Me _____	_____
3D _____	Me _____	_____
4D _____	Me _____	_____
5D _____	Me _____	_____

TEAM YEAGER
www.AprilYeager.org

Entry Log

When people ask "what do you do", your answer should be "Whatever it takes".

Rodeo ☐   Jackpot ☐

Location -

_____

Date & Time

_____

Association _____ Added Money _____ Entry Fee _____

How Many Entries _____

Balance Sheet:

Horse	Money Won	Entry Fee Per

Miles to Arena _____   Multiply by 2 _____

Vehicle Average MPG _____

Fuel Price Per Gallon _____

Hauling Partner(s) _____

Travel Cost to Show:

Enter miles to arena times 2. Divide MPG into mileage. Multiply outcome by the price per gallon. If you have hauling partners divide by that number. If you want cost per horse you can divide by the number of horses in the trailer.

$ _____   **Profit/Loss $ _____**

Stalls _____

Lodging _____

Other _____

Thankful, grateful, blessed! Doing what I love and loving what I do!!

TEAM YEAGER

www.AprilYeager.org

Preparation is EVERYTHING!

Game Plan: One barrel at a time!

Ground Conditions
_____
_____
_____

GATE:
Center Alley ☐   Right Entry ☐   Left Entry ☐

Notes: _____
_____
_____
_____

Equipment Used:
_____
_____
_____

Results: **My Draw Numbers**

1D _____	Me _____	_____
2D _____	Me _____	_____
3D _____	Me _____	_____
4D _____	Me _____	_____
5D _____	Me _____	_____

TEAM YEAGER
www.AprilYeager.org

Entry Log

When people ask "what do you do", your answer should be "Whatever it takes".

Rodeo ☐   Jackpot ☐

Location -

_____
Date & Time
_____
Association _____ Added Money _____ Entry Fee _____
How Many Entries _____

Balance Sheet:

Horse	Money Won	Entry Fee Per

Miles to Arena_____   Multiply by 2_____
Vehicle Average MPG_____
Fuel Price Per Gallon_____
Hauling Partner(s)_____
Travel Cost to Show:

Enter miles to arena times 2. Divide MPG into mileage. Multiply outcome by the price per gallon. If you have hauling partners divide by that number. If you want cost per horse you can divide by the number of horses in the trailer.

_$_____   **Profit/Loss $_____**

Stalls _____
Lodging _____
Other _____

Thankful, grateful, blessed! Doing what I love and loving what I do!!

TEAM YEAGER
www.AprilYeager.org

Preparation is EVERYTHING!

Game Plan: One barrel at a time!

Ground Conditions
_____
_____
_____

GATE:
Center Alley ☐　　Right Entry ☐　　Left Entry ☐

Notes: _____
_____
_____
_____

Equipment Used:
_____
_____
_____

Results:　　　　　　　　　　　　　　**My Draw Numbers**

1D _____	Me _____	_____
2D _____	Me _____	_____
3D _____	Me _____	_____
4D _____	Me _____	_____
5D _____	Me _____	_____

TEAM YEAGER
www.AprilYeager.org

Entry Log

When people ask "what do you do", your answer should be "Whatever it takes".

Rodeo ☐   Jackpot ☐

Location -
_____
Date & Time
_____
Association _____ Added Money _____ Entry Fee _____
How Many Entries _____

Balance Sheet:

Horse	Money Won	Entry Fee Per

Miles to Arena _____   Multiply by 2 _____
Vehicle Average MPG _____
Fuel Price Per Gallon _____
Hauling Partner(s) _____
Travel Cost to Show:
Enter miles to arena times 2. Divide MPG into mileage. Multiply outcome by the price per gallon. If you have hauling partners divide by that number. If you want cost per horse you can divide by the number of horses in the trailer.

 $_____   **Profit/Loss $_____**
Stalls _____
Lodging _____
Other _____

Thankful, grateful, blessed! Doing what I love and loving what I do!!

TEAM YEAGER
www.AprilYeager.org

Preparation is EVERYTHING!

Game Plan: One barrel at a time!

Ground Conditions
_____
_____
_____

GATE:
Center Alley ☐   Right Entry ☐   Left Entry ☐

Notes: _____
_____
_____
_____

Equipment Used:
_____
_____
_____

Results: **My Draw Numbers**

1D _____	Me _____	_____
2D _____	Me _____	_____
3D _____	Me _____	_____
4D _____	Me _____	_____
5D _____	Me _____	_____

TEAM YEAGER
www.AprilYeager.org

Entry Log

When people ask "what do you do", your answer should be "Whatever it takes".

Rodeo ☐ Jackpot ☐

Location - _____

Date & Time

_____

Association _____ Added Money _____ Entry Fee _____
How Many Entries _____

Balance Sheet:

Horse	Money Won	Entry Fee Per

Miles to Arena _____ Multiply by 2 _____
Vehicle Average MPG _____
Fuel Price Per Gallon _____
Hauling Partner(s) _____
Travel Cost to Show:
Enter miles to arena times 2. Divide MPG into mileage. Multiply outcome by the price per gallon. If you have hauling partners divide by that number. If you want cost per horse you can divide by the number of horses in the trailer.

$_____ **Profit/Loss $_____**
Stalls _____
Lodging _____
Other _____

Thankful, grateful, blessed! Doing what I love and loving what I do!!

TEAM YEAGER
www.AprilYeager.org

Preparation is EVERYTHING!

Game Plan: One barrel at a time!

Ground Conditions
_____
_____
_____

GATE:
Center Alley ☐   Right Entry ☐   Left Entry ☐

Notes: _____
_____
_____
_____

Equipment Used:
_____
_____
_____

Results: **My Draw Numbers**

1D _____	Me _____	_____
2D _____	Me _____	_____
3D _____	Me _____	_____
4D _____	Me _____	_____
5D _____	Me _____	_____

TEAM YEAGER
www.AprilYeager.org

Entry Log

When people ask "what do you do", your answer should be "Whatever it takes".

Rodeo ☐   Jackpot ☐

Location -
_____

Date & Time
_____

Association _____ Added Money _____ Entry Fee _____
How Many Entries _____

Balance Sheet:

Horse	Money Won	Entry Fee Per

Miles to Arena _____   Multiply by 2 _____
Vehicle Average MPG _____
Fuel Price Per Gallon _____
Hauling Partner(s) _____
Travel Cost to Show:
Enter miles to arena times 2. Divide MPG into mileage. Multiply outcome by the price per gallon. If you have hauling partners divide by that number. If you want cost per horse you can divide by the number of horses in the trailer.

$_____   **Profit/Loss** $_____
Stalls _____
Lodging _____
Other _____

Thankful, grateful, blessed! Doing what I love and loving what I do!!

TEAM YEAGER
www.AprilYeager.org

Preparation is EVERYTHING!

Game Plan: One barrel at a time!

Ground Conditions
_____
_____
_____

GATE:
Center Alley ☐   Right Entry ☐   Left Entry ☐

Notes: _____
_____
_____
_____

Equipment Used:
_____
_____
_____

Results: **My Draw Numbers**

1D _____   Me _____   _____
2D _____   Me _____   _____
3D _____   Me _____   _____
4D _____   Me _____   _____
5D _____   Me _____   _____

TEAM YEAGER
www.AprilYeager.org

Entry Log

When people ask "what do you do", your answer should be "Whatever it takes".

Rodeo ☐ Jackpot ☐

Location -
_____
Date & Time
_____
Association _____ Added Money _____ Entry Fee _____
How Many Entries _____

Balance Sheet:

Horse	Money Won	Entry Fee Per

Miles to Arena _____ Multiply by 2 _____
Vehicle Average MPG _____
Fuel Price Per Gallon _____
Hauling Partner(s) _____
Travel Cost to Show:

Enter miles to arena times 2. Divide MPG into mileage. Multiply outcome by the price per gallon. If you have hauling partners divide by that number. If you want cost per horse you can divide by the number of horses in the trailer.

$_____   **Profit/Loss** $_____
Stalls _____
Lodging _____
Other _____

Thankful, grateful, blessed! Doing what I love and loving what I do!!

TEAM YEAGER
www.AprilYeager.org

Preparation is EVERYTHING!

Game Plan: One barrel at a time!

Ground Conditions
_____
_____
_____

GATE:
Center Alley ☐   Right Entry ☐   Left Entry ☐

Notes: _____
_____
_____
_____

Equipment Used:
_____
_____
_____

Results: **My Draw Numbers**

1D _____	Me _____	_____
2D _____	Me _____	_____
3D _____	Me _____	_____
4D _____	Me _____	_____
5D _____	Me _____	_____

TEAM YEAGER
www.AprilYeager.org

Entry Log

When people ask "what do you do", your answer should be "Whatever it takes".

Rodeo ☐   Jackpot ☐

Location -
_____
Date & Time
_____
Association _____ Added Money _____ Entry Fee _____
How Many Entries _____

Balance Sheet:

Horse	Money Won	Entry Fee Per

Miles to Arena _____   Multiply by 2 _____
Vehicle Average MPG _____
Fuel Price Per Gallon _____
Hauling Partner(s) _____
Travel Cost to Show:

Enter miles to arena times 2. Divide MPG into mileage. Multiply outcome by the price per gallon. If you have hauling partners divide by that number. If you want cost per horse you can divide by the number of horses in the trailer.

$_____   **Profit/Loss $_____**

Stalls _____
Lodging _____
Other _____

Thankful, grateful, blessed! Doing what I love and loving what I do!!

TEAM YEAGER
www.AprilYeager.org

Preparation is EVERYTHING!

Game Plan: One barrel at a time!

Ground Conditions
_____
_____
_____

GATE:
Center Alley ☐   Right Entry ☐   Left Entry ☐
Notes: _____
_____
_____
_____

Equipment Used:
_____
_____
_____

Results: **My Draw Numbers**

1D _____	Me _____	_____
2D _____	Me _____	_____
3D _____	Me _____	_____
4D _____	Me _____	_____
5D _____	Me _____	_____

Rodeo ☐   Jackpot ☐

TEAM YEAGER
www.AprilYeager.org

Entry Log

When people ask "what do you do", your answer should be "Whatever it takes".

Location -
_____

Date & Time
_____

Association _____ Added Money _____ Entry Fee _____
How Many Entries _____

Balance Sheet:

Horse	Money Won	Entry Fee Per

Miles to Arena _____ Multiply by 2 _____
Vehicle Average MPG _____
Fuel Price Per Gallon _____
Hauling Partner(s) _____

Travel Cost to Show:

Enter miles to arena times 2. Divide MPG into mileage. Multiply outcome by the price per gallon. If you have hauling partners divide by that number. If you want cost per horse you can divide by the number of horses in the trailer.

$_____   **Profit/Loss $_____**
Stalls _____
Lodging_____
Other _____

Thankful, grateful, blessed! Doing what I love and loving what I do!!

TEAM YEAGER
www.AprilYeager.org

Preparation is EVERYTHING!

Game Plan: One barrel at a time!

Ground Conditions
_____
_____
_____

GATE:
Center Alley ☐   Right Entry ☐   Left Entry ☐

Notes:_____
_____
_____
_____

Equipment Used:
_____
_____
_____

Results: **My Draw Numbers**

1D _____   Me _____   _____
2D _____   Me _____   _____
3D _____   Me _____   _____
4D _____   Me _____   _____
5D _____   Me _____   _____

TEAM YEAGER
www.AprilYeager.org

Entry Log

When people ask "what do you do", your answer should be "Whatever it takes".

Rodeo ☐   Jackpot ☐

Location -

_____

Date & Time

_____

Association _____ Added Money _____ Entry Fee _____

How Many Entries _____

Balance Sheet:

Horse	Money Won	Entry Fee Per

Miles to Arena _____   Multiply by 2 _____

Vehicle Average MPG _____

Fuel Price Per Gallon _____

Hauling Partner(s) _____

Travel Cost to Show:

Enter miles to arena times 2. Divide MPG into mileage. Multiply outcome by the price per gallon. If you have hauling partners divide by that number. If you want cost per horse you can divide by the number of horses in the trailer.

$_____   **Profit/Loss** $_____

Stalls _____

Lodging _____

Other _____

Thankful, grateful, blessed! Doing what I love and loving what I do!!

TEAM YEAGER

www.AprilYeager.org

Preparation is EVERYTHING!

Game Plan: One barrel at a time!

Ground Conditions
_____
_____
_____

GATE:
Center Alley ☐   Right Entry ☐   Left Entry ☐

Notes: _____
_____
_____
_____

Equipment Used:
_____
_____
_____

Results: **My Draw Numbers**

1D _____	Me _____	_____
2D _____	Me _____	_____
3D _____	Me _____	_____
4D _____	Me _____	_____
5D _____	Me _____	_____

TEAM YEAGER
www.AprilYeager.org

Entry Log

When people ask "what do you do", your answer should be "Whatever it takes".

Rodeo ☐ Jackpot ☐

Location -

_____
Date & Time

_____
Association _____ Added Money _____ Entry Fee _____
How Many Entries _____

Balance Sheet:

Horse	Money Won	Entry Fee Per

Miles to Arena _____ Multiply by 2 _____
Vehicle Average MPG _____
Fuel Price Per Gallon _____
Hauling Partner(s) _____
Travel Cost to Show:

Enter miles to arena times 2. Divide MPG into mileage. Multiply outcome by the price per gallon. If you have hauling partners divide by that number. If you want cost per horse you can divide by the number of horses in the trailer.

$_____ **Profit/Loss $_____**

Stalls _____
Lodging _____
Other _____

Thankful, grateful, blessed! Doing what I love and loving what I do!!

TEAM YEAGER
www.AprilYeager.org

Preparation is EVERYTHING!

Game Plan: One barrel at a time!

Ground Conditions
_____
_____
_____

GATE:
Center Alley ☐   Right Entry ☐   Left Entry ☐

Notes: _____
_____
_____
_____

Equipment Used:
_____
_____
_____

Results: **My Draw Numbers**

1D _____	Me _____	_____
2D _____	Me _____	_____
3D _____	Me _____	_____
4D _____	Me _____	_____
5D _____	Me _____	

TEAM YEAGER
www.AprilYeager.org

Entry Log

When people ask "what do you do", your answer should be "Whatever it takes".

Rodeo ☐ Jackpot ☐

Location -
_____
Date & Time

_____
Association _____ Added Money _____ Entry Fee _____
How Many Entries _____

Balance Sheet:

Horse	Money Won	Entry Fee Per

Miles to Arena _____ Multiply by 2 _____
Vehicle Average MPG _____
Fuel Price Per Gallon _____
Hauling Partner(s) _____
Travel Cost to Show:

Enter miles to arena times 2. Divide MPG into mileage. Multiply outcome by the price per gallon. If you have hauling partners divide by that number. If you want cost per horse you can divide by the number of horses in the trailer.

$_____   **Profit/Loss $_____**

Stalls _____
Lodging _____
Other _____

Thankful, grateful, blessed! Doing what I love and loving what I do!!

TEAM YEAGER
www.AprilYeager.org

Preparation is EVERYTHING!

Ground Conditions
_____
_____
_____

Game Plan: One barrel at a time!

GATE:
Center Alley ☐   Right Entry ☐   Left Entry ☐

Notes: _____
_____
_____
_____

Equipment Used:
_____
_____
_____

Results: **My Draw Numbers**

1D _____	Me _____	_____
2D _____	Me _____	_____
3D _____	Me _____	_____
4D _____	Me _____	_____
5D _____	Me _____	

TEAM YEAGER
www.AprilYeager.org

Entry Log

When people ask "what do you do", your answer should be "Whatever it takes".

Rodeo ☐   Jackpot ☐

Location -
_____
Date & Time
_____
Association _____ Added Money _____ Entry Fee _____
How Many Entries _____

Balance Sheet:

Horse	Money Won	Entry Fee Per

Miles to Arena _____   Multiply by 2 _____
Vehicle Average MPG _____
Fuel Price Per Gallon _____
Hauling Partner(s) _____
Travel Cost to Show:

Enter miles to arena times 2. Divide MPG into mileage. Multiply outcome by the price per gallon. If you have hauling partners divide by that number. If you want cost per horse you can divide by the number of horses in the trailer.

$_____   **Profit/Loss $_____**
Stalls _____
Lodging _____
Other _____

Thankful, grateful, blessed! Doing what I love and loving what I do!!

TEAM YEAGER
www.AprilYeager.org

Preparation is EVERYTHING!

Ground Conditions
_____
_____
_____

Game Plan: One barrel at a time!

GATE:
Center Alley ☐   Right Entry ☐   Left Entry ☐

Notes:_____
_____
_____
_____

Equipment Used:
_____
_____
_____

Results: **My Draw Numbers**

1D _____	Me _____	_____
2D _____	Me _____	_____
3D _____	Me _____	_____
4D _____	Me _____	_____
5D _____	Me _____	_____

TEAM YEAGER
www.AprilYeager.org

Entry Log

When people ask "what do you do", your answer should be "Whatever it takes".

Rodeo ☐   Jackpot ☐

Location -
_____
Date & Time
_____
Association _____ Added Money _____ Entry Fee _____
How Many Entries _____

Balance Sheet:

Horse	Money Won	Entry Fee Per

Miles to Arena _____   Multiply by 2 _____
Vehicle Average MPG _____
Fuel Price Per Gallon _____
Hauling Partner(s) _____
Travel Cost to Show:
Enter miles to arena times 2. Divide MPG into mileage. Multiply outcome by the price per gallon. If you have hauling partners divide by that number. If you want cost per horse you can divide by the number of horses in the trailer.

$_____   **Profit/Loss $_____**

Stalls _____
Lodging _____
Other _____

Thankful, grateful, blessed! Doing what I love and loving what I do!!

TEAM YEAGER
www.AprilYeager.org

Preparation is EVERYTHING!

Game Plan: One barrel at a time!

Ground Conditions
_____
_____
_____

GATE:
Center Alley ☐   Right Entry ☐   Left Entry ☐

Notes: _____
_____
_____
_____

Equipment Used:
_____
_____
_____

Results: **My Draw Numbers**

1D _____	Me _____	_____
2D _____	Me _____	_____
3D _____	Me _____	_____
4D _____	Me _____	_____
5D _____	Me _____	_____

TEAM YEAGER
www.AprilYeager.org

Entry Log

When people ask "what do you do", your answer should be "Whatever it takes".

Rodeo ☐   Jackpot ☐

Location -

_____
Date & Time

_____
Association _____ Added Money _____ Entry Fee _____
How Many Entries _____

Balance Sheet:

Horse	Money Won	Entry Fee Per

Miles to Arena _____   Multiply by 2 _____
Vehicle Average MPG _____
Fuel Price Per Gallon _____
Hauling Partner(s) _____
Travel Cost to Show:
Enter miles to arena times 2. Divide MPG into mileage. Multiply outcome by the price per gallon. If you have hauling partners divide by that number. If you want cost per horse you can divide by the number of horses in the trailer.

$_____   **Profit/Loss $_____**
Stalls _____
Lodging _____
Other _____

Thankful, grateful, blessed! Doing what I love and loving what I do!!

TEAM YEAGER
www.AprilYeager.org

Preparation is EVERYTHING!

There's a difference between
INTEREST and **COMMITMENT**
When you're interested in doing something, you do it only when it's convenient.
When you're committed to something you accept no excuses; ONLY RESULTS

Kenneth Blanchard

TEAM YEAGER
www.AprilYeager.org

Entry Log

When people ask "what do you do", your answer should be "Whatever it takes".

Date:

_____
_____
_____
_____

Date:

_____
_____
_____
_____

Date:

_____
_____
_____
_____

Date:

_____
_____
_____
_____

TEAM YEAGER
www.AprilYeager.org

Preparation is EVERYTHING!

Date:

_____
_____
_____

Date:

_____
_____
_____

Date:

_____
_____
_____

Date:

_____
_____
_____

TEAM YEAGER
www.AprilYeager.org

Entry Log

When people ask "what do you do", your answer should be "Whatever it takes".

Date:
_____
_____
_____

Date:
_____
_____
_____

Date:
_____
_____
_____

Date:
_____
_____
_____

TEAM YEAGER
www.AprilYeager.org

Preparation is EVERYTHING!

Date:

_____
_____
_____

Date:

_____
_____
_____

Date:

_____
_____
_____

Date:

_____
_____
_____

TEAM YEAGER
www.AprilYeager.org

Entry Log

When people ask "what do you do", your answer should be "Whatever it takes".

Date:

_____
_____
_____
_____

Date:

_____
_____
_____
_____

Date:

_____
_____
_____
_____

Date:

_____
_____
_____
_____

TEAM YEAGER
www.AprilYeager.org

Preparation is EVERYTHING!

Date:

_____
_____
_____

Date:

_____
_____
_____

Date:

_____
_____
_____

Date:

_____
_____
_____

TEAM YEAGER
www.AprilYeager.org

Entry Log

When people ask "what do you do", your answer should be "Whatever it takes".

Date:

_____
_____
_____

Date:

_____
_____
_____

Date:

_____
_____
_____

Date:

_____
_____
_____

TEAM YEAGER
www.AprilYeager.org

Preparation is EVERYTHING!

Date:

_____
_____
_____

Date:

_____
_____
_____

Date:

_____
_____
_____

Date:

_____
_____
_____

TEAM YEAGER
www.AprilYeager.org

Entry Log

When people ask "what do you do", your answer should be "Whatever it takes".

Date:

_____
_____
_____

Date:

_____
_____
_____
_____

Date:

_____
_____
_____
_____

Date:

_____
_____
_____
_____

TEAM YEAGER
www.AprilYeager.org

Preparation is EVERYTHING!

Date:

_____
_____
_____

Date:

_____
_____
_____

Date:

_____
_____
_____

Date:

_____
_____
_____

TEAM YEAGER
www.AprilYeager.org

Entry Log

When people ask "what do you do", your answer should be "Whatever it takes".

Date:

_____
_____
_____

Date:

_____
_____
_____

Date:

_____
_____
_____

Date:

_____
_____
_____

TEAM YEAGER
www.AprilYeager.org

Preparation is EVERYTHING!

Date:

_____
_____
_____

Date:

_____
_____
_____

Date:

_____
_____
_____

Date:

_____
_____
_____

TEAM YEAGER
www.AprilYeager.org

Entry Log

When people ask "what do you do", your answer should be "Whatever it takes".

Date:

_____
_____
_____
_____

Date:

_____
_____
_____
_____

Date:

_____
_____
_____
_____

Date:

_____
_____
_____
_____

TEAM YEAGER
www.AprilYeager.org

Preparation is EVERYTHING!

Date:

_____
_____
_____

Date:

_____
_____
_____

Date:

_____
_____
_____

Date:

_____
_____
_____

TEAM YEAGER
www.AprilYeager.org

Entry Log

When people ask "what do you do", your answer should be "Whatever it takes".

Date:

_____
_____
_____
_____

Date:

_____
_____
_____
_____

Date:

_____
_____
_____
_____

Date:

_____
_____
_____
_____

TEAM YEAGER
www.AprilYeager.org

Preparation is EVERYTHING!

Date:

_____
_____
_____

Date:

_____
_____
_____

Date:

_____
_____
_____

Date:

_____
_____
_____

TEAM YEAGER
www.AprilYeager.org

Entry Log

When people ask "what do you do", your answer should be "Whatever it takes".

Date:

_____
_____
_____

Date:

_____
_____
_____

Date:

_____
_____
_____

Date:

_____
_____
_____

TEAM YEAGER
www.AprilYeager.org

Preparation is EVERYTHING!

Date:

_____
_____
_____

Date:

_____
_____
_____

Date:

_____
_____
_____

Date:

_____
_____
_____

TEAM YEAGER
www.AprilYeager.org

Entry Log

When people ask "what do you do", your answer should be "Whatever it takes".

Date:

_____
_____
_____

Date:

_____
_____
_____

Date:

_____
_____
_____

Date:

_____
_____
_____

TEAM YEAGER
www.AprilYeager.org

Preparation is EVERYTHING!

Date:

_____
_____
_____

Date:

_____
_____
_____

Date:

_____
_____
_____

Date:

_____
_____
_____

TEAM YEAGER
www.AprilYeager.org

Entry Log

When people ask "what do you do", your answer should be "Whatever it takes".

Date:

_____
_____
_____

Date:

_____
_____
_____

Date:

_____
_____
_____

Date:

_____
_____
_____

TEAM YEAGER
www.AprilYeager.org

Preparation is EVERYTHING!

Date:

_____
_____
_____

Date:

_____
_____
_____

Date:

_____
_____
_____

Date:

_____
_____
_____

TEAM YEAGER
www.AprilYeager.org

Entry Log

When people ask "what do you do", your answer should be "Whatever it takes".

Date:

_____
_____
_____

Date:

_____
_____
_____

Date:

_____
_____
_____

Date:

_____
_____
_____

TEAM YEAGER
www.AprilYeager.org

Preparation is EVERYTHING!

Date:

_____
_____
_____

Date:

_____
_____
_____

Date:

_____
_____
_____

Date:

_____
_____
_____

TEAM YEAGER
www.AprilYeager.org

Entry Log

When people ask "what do you do", your answer should be "Whatever it takes".

Date:
_____
_____
_____

Date:
_____
_____
_____

Date:
_____
_____
_____

Date:
_____
_____
_____

TEAM YEAGER
www.AprilYeager.org

Preparation is EVERYTHING!

Date:

_____
_____
_____

Date:

_____
_____
_____

Date:

_____
_____
_____

Date:

_____
_____
_____

TEAM YEAGER
www.AprilYeager.org

Entry Log

When people ask "what do you do", your answer should be "Whatever it takes".

Date:

_____
_____
_____
_____

Date:

_____
_____
_____
_____

Date:

_____
_____
_____
_____

Date:

_____
_____
_____
_____

TEAM YEAGER
www.AprilYeager.org

Preparation is EVERYTHING!

Date:

_____
_____
_____

Date:

_____
_____
_____

Date:

_____
_____
_____

Date:

_____
_____
_____

TEAM YEAGER
www.AprilYeager.org

Entry Log

When people ask "what do you do", your answer should be "Whatever it takes".

Date:

_____
_____
_____

Date:

_____
_____
_____

Date:

_____
_____
_____

Date:

_____
_____
_____

TEAM YEAGER
www.AprilYeager.org

Preparation is EVERYTHING!

Date:

_____
_____
_____

Date:

_____
_____
_____

Date:

_____
_____
_____

Date:

_____
_____
_____

TEAM YEAGER
www.AprilYeager.org

Entry Log

When people ask "what do you do", your answer should be "Whatever it takes".

Date:
_____
_____
_____

Date:
_____
_____
_____

Date:
_____
_____
_____

Date:
_____
_____
_____

TEAM YEAGER
www.AprilYeager.org

Preparation is EVERYTHING!

Date:

_____
_____
_____

Date:

_____
_____
_____
_____

Date:

_____
_____
_____
_____

Date:

_____
_____
_____
_____

TEAM YEAGER
www.AprilYeager.org

Entry Log

When people ask "what do you do", your answer should be "Whatever it takes".

Date:

_____
_____
_____

Date:

_____
_____
_____
_____

Date:

_____
_____
_____
_____

Date:

_____
_____
_____
_____

TEAM YEAGER
www.AprilYeager.org

Preparation is EVERYTHING!

Date:

_____
_____
_____

Date:

_____
_____
_____

Date:

_____
_____
_____

Date:

_____
_____
_____

TEAM YEAGER
www.AprilYeager.org

Entry Log

When people ask "what do you do", your answer should be "Whatever it takes".

Date:
_____
_____
_____

Date:
_____
_____
_____
_____

Date:
_____
_____
_____

Date:
_____
_____
_____
_____

TEAM YEAGER
www.AprilYeager.org

Preparation is EVERYTHING!

Date:

_____
_____
_____

Date:

_____
_____
_____

Date:

_____
_____
_____

Date:

_____
_____
_____

TEAM YEAGER
www.AprilYeager.org

Entry Log

When people ask "what do you do", your answer should be "Whatever it takes".

Date:
_____
_____
_____

Date:
_____
_____
_____

Date:
_____
_____
_____

Date:
_____
_____
_____

TEAM YEAGER
www.AprilYeager.org

Preparation is EVERYTHING!

Date:

_____
_____
_____

Date:

_____
_____
_____

Date:

_____
_____
_____

Date:

_____
_____
_____

TEAM YEAGER
www.AprilYeager.org

Entry Log

When people ask "what do you do", your answer should be "Whatever it takes".

Date:

_____
_____
_____

Date:

_____
_____
_____

Date:

_____
_____
_____

Date:

_____
_____
_____

TEAM YEAGER
www.AprilYeager.org

Preparation is EVERYTHING!

Date:

_____
_____
_____

Date:

_____
_____
_____

Date:

_____
_____
_____

Date:

_____
_____
_____

TEAM YEAGER
www.AprilYeager.org

Entry Log

When people ask "what do you do", your answer should be "Whatever it takes".

Date:

_____
_____
_____
_____

Date:

_____
_____
_____
_____

Date:

_____
_____
_____
_____

Date:

_____
_____
_____
_____

TEAM YEAGER
www.AprilYeager.org

Preparation is EVERYTHING!

Date:

_____
_____
_____

Date:

_____
_____
_____

Date:

_____
_____
_____

Date:

_____
_____
_____

TEAM YEAGER
www.AprilYeager.org

Entry Log

When people ask "what do you do", your answer should be "Whatever it takes".

Date:

_____
_____
_____
_____

Date:

_____
_____
_____
_____

Date:

_____
_____
_____
_____

Date:

_____
_____
_____
_____

TEAM YEAGER
www.AprilYeager.org

Preparation is EVERYTHING!

Date:

_____
_____
_____

Date:

_____
_____
_____

Date:

_____
_____
_____

Date:

_____
_____
_____

TEAM YEAGER
www.AprilYeager.org

Entry Log

When people ask "what do you do", your answer should be "Whatever it takes".

Date:
_____
_____
_____

Date:
_____
_____
_____

Date:
_____
_____
_____

Date:
_____
_____
_____

TEAM YEAGER
www.AprilYeager.org

Preparation is EVERYTHING!

Date:

_____
_____
_____

Date:

_____
_____
_____

Date:

_____
_____
_____

Date:

_____
_____
_____

TEAM YEAGER
www.AprilYeager.org

Entry Log

When people ask "what do you do", your answer should be "Whatever it takes".

Date:

_____
_____
_____

Date:

_____
_____
_____
_____

Date:

_____
_____
_____

Date:

_____
_____
_____
_____

TEAM YEAGER
www.AprilYeager.org

Preparation is EVERYTHING!

Date:

_____
_____
_____

Date:

_____
_____
_____

Date:

_____
_____
_____

Date:

_____
_____
_____

TEAM YEAGER
www.AprilYeager.org

Entry Log

When people ask "what do you do", your answer should be "Whatever it takes".

Date:

_____
_____
_____
_____

Date:

_____
_____
_____
_____

Date:

_____
_____
_____
_____

Date:

_____
_____
_____
_____

TEAM YEAGER
www.AprilYeager.org

Preparation is EVERYTHING!

Date:

_____
_____
_____

Date:

_____
_____
_____

Date:

_____
_____
_____

Date:

_____
_____
_____

TEAM YEAGER
www.AprilYeager.org

Entry Log

When people ask "what do you do", your answer should be "Whatever it takes".

Date:

_____
_____
_____

Date:

_____
_____
_____
_____

Date:

_____
_____
_____
_____

Date:

_____
_____
_____
_____

TEAM YEAGER
www.AprilYeager.org

Preparation is EVERYTHING!

Date:

_____
_____
_____

Date:

_____
_____
_____

Date:

_____
_____
_____

Date:

_____
_____
_____

TEAM YEAGER
www.AprilYeager.org

Entry Log

When people ask "what do you do", your answer should be "Whatever it takes".

Date:

_____
_____
_____

Date:

_____
_____
_____

Date:

_____
_____
_____

Date:

_____
_____
_____

TEAM YEAGER
www.AprilYeager.org

Preparation is EVERYTHING!

Date:

_____
_____
_____

Date:

_____
_____
_____

Date:

_____
_____
_____

Date:

_____
_____
_____

TEAM YEAGER
www.AprilYeager.org

Entry Log

When people ask "what do you do", your answer should be "Whatever it takes".

Date:

_____
_____
_____

Date:

_____
_____
_____

Date:

_____
_____
_____

Date:

_____
_____
_____

TEAM YEAGER
www.AprilYeager.org

Preparation is EVERYTHING!

Date:

_____
_____
_____

Date:

_____
_____
_____

Date:

_____
_____
_____

Date:

_____
_____
_____

TEAM YEAGER
www.AprilYeager.org

Entry Log

When people ask "what do you do", your answer should be "Whatever it takes".

Date:
_____
_____
_____

Date:
_____
_____
_____

Date:
_____
_____
_____

Date:
_____
_____
_____

TEAM YEAGER
www.AprilYeager.org

Preparation is EVERYTHING!

Date:

_____
_____
_____

Date:

_____
_____
_____

Date:

_____
_____
_____

Date:

_____
_____
_____
_____

TEAM YEAGER
www.AprilYeager.org

Made in the USA
Lexington, KY
28 August 2018